D0403079

chapter one

Dining Dos and Don'ts

*W*hether you are eating in the American or Continental style, with two courses, four courses, or seven, here is a summary of dining dos and don'ts to help you finesse any meal.

THE DOS

❧ Do try a little of everything served to

The
Little Book of
Etiquette

By Dorothea Johnson

RUNNING PRESS

PHILADELPHIA • LONDON

A Running Press Miniature Edition™

Library of Congress Cataloging-in-Publication Number 96-69226

ISBN 0-7624-0009-9

This book may be ordered by mail from the publisher.
Please include $1.00 for postage and handling.
But try your bookstore first!

Running Press Book Publishers
125 South Twenty-second Street
Philadelphia, Pennsylvania 19103-4399

Contents

Introduction

"The world was my oyster, but I used the wrong fork," Oscar Wilde said more than one hundred years ago. In 1994, Harvey Mackay, author of *Swim with the Sharks*, stressed the importance of etiquette in today's world: "They don't teach etiquette much anymore, but if you ever have to choose between Incredibly

Advanced Accounting for Overachievers and Remedial Fork and Knife, head for the silverware."

　𝒯oday, business is the largest social environment in the world. Our rapidly expanding global economy forces us to socialize and conduct business at the table more than ever before. It is in this setting that table manners play a major role as relationships are developed and strengthened. There is no better, or possibly worse, place to make an impression.

Good table manners, however, aren't just for those in the business arena. Every one of us can benefit from a good dose of etiquette training. Good manners make us more pleasant to be around. After all, no one enjoys dining with a person who has yet to learn not to chew with an open mouth.

Let's face it: We are judged by our table manners and we judge others by their table manners. Persons sitting at or near our table cannot help but notice our table manners or lack of them. If our table manners are good, they will judge us favorably; and if our table manners are poor, they will judge us unfavorably.

Fortunately, the rules of dining etiquette are straightforward and easy to master. Some of them have been devised for the safety of the diner, while others make eating look more attractive. To some extent usage is codified to help things run more smoothly. The noted zoologist Dr. Konrad Lorenz has pointed out that most animals, even the irresponsible crow, have rules of protocol and decorum. Crows, with a minimum of squabbling and flapping, arrange themselves on a telephone wire in order of precedence from right to left. Knowing the correct way to handle any situation, even a telephone wire, makes life less confusing.

This guide will take you step-by-step through the elements of dining as you acquire the skills that elevate your demeanor from mere eating to fine dining.

My goals are not to teach you how to set a proper table but to guide you in managing a table that has already been set. While you may need to unlearn some bad habits, the rewards are impressive. You will be at ease as a guest or as a host in business and social arenas worldwide.

❧ Do look into, not over, your cup or glass when drinking.

❧ Do remember your posture at the table. Sit up straight and keep your arms (including elbows) off the table.

❧ Do take medicine discreetly, preferably away from the table. If you must take medication at the table, do not mention it to anyone.

❧ Do remove alien objects from your mouth with your fingers and place them at the edge of your plate.

you unless you know you are allergic to it.

⚘ Do avoid talking with your mouth full. Take small bites and you will find it is easier to answer questions and join in table talk.

⚘ Do wait until you have swallowed the food in your mouth before you take a sip of your beverage.

⚘ Do take a quick sip of water if a bite of food is too hot.

⚘ Do carry food to your mouth with an inward, not an outward, curve of the fork or spoon.

☙ DON'T blow on food that is hot. Wait until it cools. Eat soup from the side of the soup plate or bowl first, where it cools the fastest.

☙ DON'T crumble crackers in your soup. Oyster crackers are scattered, a few at a time, into the oyster stew.

☙ DON'T tell the other diners you need to use the restroom. Quietly say "Excuse me," place your napkin on the chair seat, and slide the chair under the table.

☙ DON'T fidget and squirm. Both your feet should rest flat on the floor.

Dining Dos and Don'ts

THE DON'TS

❧ Don't overload your plate.

❧ Don't, under any circumstances, put your knife in your mouth.

❧ Don't mop your face with a napkin.

❧ Don't spread your elbows when cutting meat. Keep them close to your sides when eating.

❧ Don't saw back and forth at your meat with a knife. Stroke the knife toward you.

❧ Don't chew with your mouth open.

❧ Don't smack your lips.

❧ Don't touch your head at the table.

❧ Don't lean back in your chair. All four legs of the chair should rest on the floor.

❧ Don't reach across the table or across another person to get something. If it is out of reach, ask the closest person to pass it to you.

❧ Don't pick your teeth at the table, either with a toothpick or with your fingers. If something gets caught in your teeth, excuse yourself and take care of the problem in the privacy of the restroom.

❧ Don't push your plate away from you when you have finished eating.

❧ DON'T gesture with your fork, knife, or spoon in your hand.

❧ DON'T talk about your personal food likes and dislikes while eating.

❧ DON'T dip your fingers or napkin into the water glass to wipe off a stain. Excuse yourself and go to the restroom.

❧ DON'T complain about the food or service in front of your guests. Quietly excuse yourself and speak directly to the maître d' or manager. Guests must never complain about a problem with the food or service, but should quietly inform their host, whose duty it is to handle this matter.

☙ DON'T place personal items, such as purses, briefcases, and glasses, on the table. A small purse belongs on the lap and large purses near your feet.

☙ DON'T do any grooming at the table. Excuse yourself and go to the restroom.

☙ DON'T smoke before or during a meal. If you are seated in a smoking section, light up only after dessert is finished. In private homes and businesses, the absence of ashtrays means no smoking.

chapter two

TABLE TALK

$\mathscr{N}$ow that you know the dining dos and don'ts, the following guidelines will empower you to dine with ease by acquainting you with the subtle nuances of the table and its accoutrements.

$\mathscr{B}$efore you sit down, approach each person at the table whom you have not met beforehand. Extend your hand

and introduce yourself, greeting guests you already know by name. You can be assured everyone will remember you for taking the time to greet each diner personally.

Place cards are used at many business and social events and guests should never rearrange them. Your host has given considerable thought to where guests should sit and this placement

is usually determined by precedence according to established protocol.

To seat yourself, or to be seated by someone, move to the right of your chair and sit down from your left side. Men still pull out chairs for women, and this courtesy should be acknowledged graciously. However, professional women do not expect their male associates to seat them at business functions.

Once you are seated, study the place setting carefully. While the array of silverware before you may seem daunting, your place setting should be viewed as a map to help guide you through the meal. With a little practice, you can determine the number of courses being served by assessing the silverware at your place setting. In upscale restaurants, however, beware. The servers may replace the necessary silverware before each course.

The knives and soup spoon are placed on the right and the forks are on the left. When a seafood cocktail is served, the fork is often placed on the bowl of the soup spoon or on the plate on

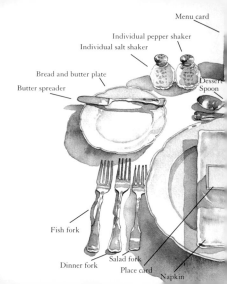

Menu card

Individual pepper shaker

Individual salt shaker

Bread and butter plate

Butter spreader

Dessert Spoon

Fish fork

Dinner fork

Salad fork

Place card

Napkin

Water goblet

Champagne flute

Red wine glass

White wine glass

Sherry glass

ssert fork

Cocktail fork

Salad knife

Dinner knife

Fish knife

Soup spoon

Place plate

which the seafood cocktail is served. Napkins are in the center of the service plate or to the left of the forks. Liquids are always on the right, and solids, such as the salad or bread and butter plate, are on the left.

Should the person on your left commandeer your bread plate, which often happens, use your dinner plate for bread and don't acknowledge the faux pas. Resist the urge to take the bread plate on your right and confuse others.

Silverware is used from the outside

in. When the salad fork and knife are placed next to the plate, this indicates that the salad will be served after the entree (main course) and before dessert. The custom of serving salad before the entree originated in California as a simple way to pacify hungry restaurant diners who demanded something to eat besides bread, hence the term "salad California style." The style is widely copied throughout the country, because many believe restaurants practice correct service. Alas, this is not always true. When the salad is served first, the salad fork is to the far left, not next to the plate as shown in the illustration on page 26.

The fork and spoon placed above the dinner plate are to be used for dessert. Should you make a mistake and pick up the wrong utensil, simply go on eating with it and ask the server to replace it for the next course.

Glasses are placed above the soup spoon and knives in the order of their use, as shown on page 27. Each is removed with the course it accompanies with the exception of the dessert wine glass, which remains through the coffee when coffee is served at the table.

The illustration on page 32 shows two of the most popular wine glasses for red and white wine. Red wines should be uncorked to allow them to breathe for an hour before serving and poured when their temperature is not less than 65 degrees. Once opened, do not recork at the table.

Chill white wines and Beaujolais thoroughly for about three to four hours or to 40 or 50 degrees Fahrenheit before serving. Fruity and sweet wines should be chilled to a lower temperature.

*W*hite wine glasses are held by the

Red
wine glass

White
wine glass

stem and red wine glasses by the bottom of the bowl when one is at a seated dinner. Leave the wine swirling, gargling, and stem maneuvers to the oenophiles.

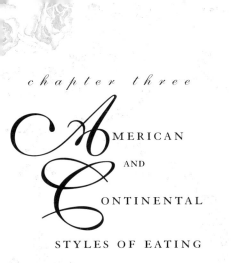

chapter three

American

and

Continental

Styles of Eating

How to Hold
Your Fork and Knife

The most important thing to know when dining is how to hold your fork and knife correctly. Grasping the fork like a cello and the knife like a dagger will place you firmly in the "silverware hall of shame." My method, shown in the illustrations and described below, will enable you to dine anyplace in the world with refinement and confidence.

Open your hands, palms up. Place the fork and knife in your open hands, as

shown. Let half of the handle of the fork
and knife rest on the palm of each hand;
the remainder
should rest on
your index
fingers.

Grasp the
fork and knife
and turn your
hands over,
resting your
index fingers
along the handles.

Until the 1840s, Americans and Europeans ate in the same style—with the fork in the right hand. In the mid-nineteenth century, however, the fashionable upper class stopped shifting their forks back and forth between their right and left hands. As more middle-class eaters learned to convey food into their mouth with tines instead of blades, the upper class hit upon this as a new class identification. It became fashionable first in England. Then in 1853 a French etiquette book described the latest mode

of dining favored by fashionable people.
Before long, all Europeans began eating
in this style.

As the year 2000 approaches, more
and more Americans are changing to the

AMERICAN

Continental style. No matter which style you use, the key is to manipulate your fork and knife with ease and confidence and to know where to place them on your plate at the end of each course.

AMERICAN

In the American style of eating, the knife is used for cutting only. It is held in the right hand (if you are left handed, reverse the process).

Hold the fork in your left hand,

CONTINENTAL

tines down. Cut with your knife, and then put it down on the edge of your plate, blade edge facing in. Switch the fork to your right hand and hold it the way a pencil is held (steadied between

CONTINENTAL

your index finger and middle finger, and secured by your thumb). Then, convey the food to your mouth.

In the Continental style of eating, the knife remains in the right hand and the fork in the left. After the food is cut, use your knife to secure it on your fork. *Both utensils remain in their respective hands.* Bring the fork, tines down, to your mouth by twisting your wrist and raising your forearm slightly.

chapter four

THE DINING TUTORIAL

On the following pages is a step-by-step guide to the most formal dining experience available here or abroad: the seven-course formal dinner. The meal consists of a soup course, a fish course, a sorbet course, a meat or fowl course, a salad course (often served with cheese), a dessert course, and a coffee course.

*O*nce you are seated at the table, pause and look around at the other diners before picking up your napkin. If you are the host, you should be the first to do so. If you are a guest, wait until your host does. In many upscale restaurants, the server will remove your napkin from the table, unfold it, and place it on your lap. Large dinner napkins are left folded in half and placed across the lap with the fold facing your waist. Smaller luncheon napkins are opened fully on your lap.

Traditional service of a meal has not changed since the late nineteenth century. The rules remain the same: Food is served from the left and removed from the right; liquids are poured and cleared from the right; and serving platters are offered from the left.

THE SOUP COURSE

The soup spoon is held the same way a fork is held (steadied between your index finger and middle finger, and secured by your thumb). Soup is spooned away from you toward the center of the soup plate and sipped from the side of the spoon. The soup plate may be tipped away from you to get the last of the soup. The spoon is placed on the soup plate between sips and when you have finished.

*W*hen soup is served in a two-handled cream soup bowl or bouillon cup, place your spoon on the underlying saucer between sips and when you have finished.

*W*ine is served with the soup course, and sherry is the choice for all consommés and any soup that is seasoned with sherry. The server will pour from the right directly into the glass resting on the table. Do not touch your glass until your host has lifted his glass, which is a signal that a few words of welcome will be said to begin the meal (see Toasting on page 64).

Should you choose not to drink wine, lightly touch your fingertips to the glass rim. You may raise an empty glass for a toast, but never turn your glass upside down to decline wine.

THE FISH COURSE

Fish forks and knives are used in most upscale restaurants. They are easy to identify because of their unusual shape.

There are slight indentations on the outermost tines of your fish fork. These indentations are for lifting the skeleton of the fish when it is served with the bones.

The blade of a fish knife is not sharp like a dinner knife because fish is tender and requires very little cutting. In addition, the point is off-center in order to aid the diner in boning a fish (see Fish on page 77).

To eat with a fish fork and knife, hold the fish fork in your left hand, tines down. The fish knife s held like a fork

(steadied between your index finger and middle finger, and secured by your thumb). Use the fish knife to cut the fish and guide it onto the back of your fork.

*Y*ou may use only the fish fork when the fish is soft and boneless. When you hold the fork in your right hand, the tines are up. If you are eating with only the fork, leave the knife on the table.

*W*hen the fish course is finished, place the fork and knife in the "finished" position. First, visualize the face of a clock on your plate. Place the fork and

knife in the approximate position of
10:20, with the tips of the fork and knife
at 10 and the handles at 20. The tines of
the fork may be placed up or down and
the blade of the knife should face the fork.

When you are pausing between

bites, use the "rest" position. Think of this as an inverted "V." Cross the fork and knife on your plate, with the fork, tines down, over the knife. The fork tines should face approximately 2 on the plate clock, and the handle should face 8. The knife tip should face 10 and the handle 4.

Each handle should extend about an inch over the rim of your plate. Don't bridge your fork and knife on the table against the edge of the plate. Once silverware is picked up by the diner, it should never touch the table again.

A highly trained server will not remove your plate with the fork and knife crossed. This is a universally known silent signal indicating the diner has not finished and is only resting. But not all restaurant professionals are trained to understand this silent service code. Should one attempt to take your plate while you are still eating, quietly say, "I have not finished."

THE SORBET COURSE

*S*orbet is served after the fish course as a palate cleanser. It is served with its own spoon on the underlying plate. You will not find this utensil on the place setting before the meal.

   Eat your sorbet from the glass or dish just as you would ice cream, leaving the spoon on the underlying plate when you are finished. The garnish may also be eaten.

THE MEAT OR FOWL COURSE

   The meat knife is not held like a fish knife because more leverage is needed for cutting. The index finger points down the handle and firmly presses down. The fork is held in the left hand, tines down, when cutting food, as shown on page 37.

Spear the meat with the fork and cut it off with the knife. Put the knife blade under the piece of meat and twist the handle slightly to secure the meat on the tines of the fork. A small amount of potatoes or vegetables may be placed on the tines of the fork with the meat. Cut only one piece at a time.

THE SALAD COURSE

Salad may be eaten with a fork and

knife just as you eat fish and meat. Leave the knife on the table if the salad can be eaten with the fork alone. When cheese is

served with the salad, use the cheese server on the platter and place a small portion of cheese on your salad plate together with crackers or bread. Use your salad knife to put cheese on crackers or bread. Place both the fork and knife in the "finished" position when you are done, even if you have only used the fork.

THE DESSERT COURSE

*First, transfer the dessert utensils from above the plate to the sides of the plate, fork on the left and spoon on the right. Dessert may be eaten with the fork in the left hand, tines down, and the

spoon in the right. Eat with the spoon
and use the fork to secure certain desserts
(such as tarts) and to use as a pusher. Eat
pie or cake only with a fork; for ice cream
or pudding, use a spoon. Leave the other
utensil in place on the table. Place the

fork and spoon in the "finished" position when you are done, even if you have used only one of them.

THE COFFEE COURSE

Coffee or demitasse may be served as a separate course with chocolates or with the dessert.

TOASTING AND CLOSING THE MEAL

It is no longer a rule that toasts be drunk with wine, nor is it considered bad luck to toast with water. Those who do not drink can raise a glass of water.

A toast is a very special honor to the person receiving it. There are two types of toasts. They are usually offered at the beginning of the meal or at the beginning of the desert course. At the beginning of the meal, the host will often remain seated and make a toast to welcome everyone. This is why a guest does not take a sip of wine that has been poured until the host does so.

At the beginning of the dessert

course, the host may propose a toast to the guest of honor. At this time, it is traditional that the host stand. The person to whom the toast is proposed should remain seated and, while he may hold a glass, should not raise it or touch it to his lips. One does not drink a toast to oneself.

The person who was toasted should then rise and respond with a toast, to which he may drink. Other guests may now rise and propose toasts of their own.

After making sure all the guests have finished eating, the host may signal that the meal is over by placing his napkin to the left of his plate. This is a signal for you to do the same. Do not refold your napkin. Pick it up from the center and place it loosely on the table to the left of your plate.

chapter five

Eating Various Foods

$\mathcal{A}$t my dining tutorials, participants always ask how to handle certain unusual or difficult foods. My first advice is to order user-friendly foods that are easy to manage with a fork and knife. This allows you to focus on your agenda rather than on solving the mysteries of challenging foods. Be your own best friend and order grilled boneless chicken breast or fish, cooked vegetables, simple cake, pies, ice cream, fruit cut in bite-size pieces, or berries.

For those occasions when you don't have a choice, when the menu is pre-selected and you must make the best of it, I offer these universally accepted techniques for eating specific foods.

ARTICHOKES—Eat with your fingers. Remove each leaf separately, dip the soft end in sauce, and then pull it through your teeth to remove the edible portion. Discard the remainder of the leaf on the side of your plate. Secure the heart with a fork and scrape the thistle away with a knife. Then cut the heart into pieces and eat it with a fork.

ASPARAGUS—Cut into bite-size portions and eat with a fork. In Europe it is eaten with the fingers. Individual asparagus tongs may also be used.

BACON—Eat with a fork and knife. Only very crisp bacon may be eaten with your fingers.

BERRIES—Eat with a spoon. Large strawberries are often served with the stem. Hold the strawberry by the stem, dip it in sugar, and eat it in one or two bites. Discard the stem on the side of your plate.

BREAD AND BUTTER—Do not pull the roll in half. Break off only one bite of your bread or roll at a time, then butter it with your butter spreader and eat. Do the buttering on your plate, not in your hand. When butter is passed, take a portion onto your butter plate with the butter server. If pats are used, pick them up with a fork and place on your plate.

CELERY, OLIVES, PICKLES, AND RADISHES—

Remove from the serving tray with your fingers and place on the side of your dinner plate or bread and butter plate. All are eaten with the fingers. Eat large olives with a pit in several bites, discarding the pit on the side of your plate. Small stuffed olives are eaten whole.

CHERRIES, KUMQUATS, AND PLUMS (RAW)—Eat with your fingers in one or two bites. The stones are dropped into the cupped hand and put on the side of the plate.

CHICKEN, DUCK, AND TURKEY—Eat with a fork and knife. Fried chicken is only eaten with the fingers at a picnic or a casual family gathering.

CLAMS AND OYSTERS (FRESH)—Use an oyster fork for oysters and clams served on the half-shell. Hold the shell with one hand and remove the oyster or clam whole with the fork. Dip it in the sauce, and eat it in one mouthful. Large oysters may be cut in half.

CORN ON THE COB—Butter and season several rows at a time, not the whole ear at once. Hold the ear firmly with both hands and eat. Corn is served only at casual meals.

EGGS—Eat hard-cooked eggs with a fork. To eat soft-cooked eggs served in an egg cup, slice off the cap with a knife and eat directly from the shell with a spoon. Soft-cooked eggs may also be scooped out of the shell into a small dish and eaten with a spoon.

FISH—Today it is rare to be served a

whole fish in America; in many European countries, however, small fish are served whole, complete with the head and tail. Hold the fish fork in your left hand and the fish knife in your right hand and bone as follows: Secure the fish with your fork and use your knife to cut off the head and tail and put them to one side of the plate. Next, cut away the edge of the fish along the stomach to remove the small bones. Repeat this process along the backbone and lift away the top filet. The backbone will then lie exposed, and

the top filet will be entirely free of bones.
When this has been eaten, slip the knife
between the other filet and the backbone.
Lift away the backbone and put it next to
the head and tail. Tiny bones may get in
your mouth. Remove them with your
thumb and index finger and place them
on the side of your plate.

LEMON—Secure a wedge of lemon with a
fork and press out the juice with your
free hand. If a slice of lemon is served,
secure the slice with a fork and press out
the juice with a knife.

LOBSTER—First crack the claws with a nutcracker. Then extract the meat with a seafood fork, dip it in butter or sauce, and eat. Cut large pieces with a fork. Pull off and clean the small claws, sucking on the ends as if you were drinking through a straw. Stuffed lobster and hardshell crabs are eaten with a fork and knife.

PASTA—To eat spaghetti, use your fork and separate a few

strands. Hold the tip of the prongs against the plate and twirl the fork around to gather the strands onto it. Don't stir and don't use a spoon. Even in Italy the use of a spoon is frowned upon except at very informal, family-style meals. Small-sized pasta such as tortellini, ziti, and penne are eaten with a fork. POTATOES—Eat baked potatoes from the skin with a fork, and then eat the skin with a fork and knife. Add butter by taking some from your butter plate with your dinner knife. Do not mash potatoes on your plate. French fries are halved and eaten with a fork. Eat chips and shoe-string potatoes with your fingers.

SANDWICHES—Tea-type sandwiches and canapés are eaten with the fingers. (A canapé is an appetizer consisting of a piece of bread or toast or a cracker topped with a savory spread.) Club sandwiches may be eaten with a fork and knife or cut into fourths and eaten with the fingers. Open-faced sandwiches are eaten with a fork and knife.

SAUCES—Sauces may be poured over or

beside meat. A forkful of food at a time may be dipped into the sauce.

SHRIMP—Cocktail shrimp are eaten with a seafood fork. Eat large shrimp in two bites. If the tails have been left on, hold the shrimp by the tail with your fingers. Dip in sauce, bite off, and discard the tail.

STEWED FRUIT—Eat with a spoon. Pits should be dropped into your spoon and placed on the side of your plate.

TORTILLAS—Place plain tortillas flat on your hand or plate. Fill, roll up, and eat from the end. Baked tortillas covered in cheese and sauce are eaten with a fork and knife.

WATER—Blot your mouth before taking a drink. Do not drink water while food is in your mouth, roll water around your mouth, or swallow loudly. If you have taken too hot a mouthful of food, sip a bit of water. Do not forcefully drain an entire glassful. Hold a tumbler-type glass near the bottom, a small stem glass by the stem, and large goblets at the bottom of the bowl.

WATERMELON—Eat with a fork unless cubed. Eat with a spoon when cut into small pieces and served in a dish. Use a fork and knife when served with the rind attached. Drop seeds into your cupped hand and place them on the side of your plate.

chapter six

FINESSING THE

BUSINESS

MEAL

The business meal is more than a straightforward dining experience because food is not the only item on the menu. A business meal may help you get to know a client better, encourage new business, or keep a good client happy. In each scenario the food may be the centerpiece, but the main course is the business agenda. There is, of course, protocol to be observed by the host and guest.

HOST DUTIES

*W*hen you are the host, you must control the entire event in order to accomplish your goals. It is your duty to handle every detail of the meal, from extending the invitation and making reservations to handling the tip and the coat check.

*I*t is important to be familiar with the restaurant you are using because you will be more comfortable in a place where you are known and where you will feel in control. Your guest will be impressed if you are greeted by name, and this only happens when you have established a rapport with the maître d'.

If the restaurant is new to you, stop in before the day of your scheduled meeting, introduce yourself to the maître d', select a table, and familiarize yourself with the menu and the surroundings. Ask management to imprint your credit card and request that the check be held at the captain's station for your signature. Or you may choose to sign the check in advance and request that management add the customary gratuity.

This advance preparation will prevent the check from being presented to you at the table. Your receipt will be handed to you discreetly as you leave the restaurant. Savvy executives of both genders are using this sophisticated method of handling the check.

The logical business meal is lunch. It is best to extend a business dinner invitation only when you know someone well, have a set agenda, and have a good reason to meet after 6:00 p.m.

Place the call yourself. A first time invitation should never be extended secretary-to-secretary. Give the purpose of your invitation so the guest can come prepared. It is not professional to invite someone to a business meal without an agenda.

Never ask a guest where he wants to eat. The burden of choice belongs to the host. But be sure to take the location of your guest's office into consideration when deciding where to eat. Select a convenient location that compliments his taste. If he is austere and rather humble, you don't want to choose the fanciest restaurant in town. On the other hand, a prospective client or established client who has entertained you lavishly deserves similar treatment.

Once you have established the date, time, and location for your meeting, ask your guest if he would prefer a seat in the smoking or non-smoking section.

If he says "Smoking please," you should honor his request unless you are allergic to smoke. If this is the case, then you should reply, "Because of my allergies, I find it necessary to sit in the non-smoking section. I hope that is agreeable with you?"

Make reservations in your name and in the name of your company to indicate that this is a business meal, and specify where you would like to sit. Choose a table that will give you maximum privacy, one that doesn't face a mirror and is as far away from the kitchen and restrooms as possible.

The day before a business lunch, reconfirm your reservation with the restaurant, eliminating the possibility of the restaurant having no record of it. Then confirm the appointment with your guest. A breakfast meeting should be confirmed the afternoon before. In this case, you should provide your guest with your home telephone number in case an emergency arises. If the meeting is canceled, call the restaurant to let them know. No-shows are not appreciated in the restaurant arena.

Arrive at least fifteen minutes before the agreed-upon time, check the table, and if you didn't handle this ahead of time, arrange payment of the check with the captain or maître d'. Confirming these details empowers you to maintain complete control while you are hosting. No one—the maître d', captain, servers, or anyone else in the restaurant—should doubt that you are the host.

If you find at the last moment that

you are running late, call the restaurant and ask the maître d' to see that your dining companion is greeted and advised that you will be detained briefly. Leave instructions for your guest to be seated at your table and invited to order a drink.

*W*hen your guest is not on time, wait about fifteen minutes before calling to find out why he or she has not arrived. Unless you can be assured that your guest will arrive, wait thirty minutes past the agreed-upon time. Then you may order or leave. Should you decide not to stay, it is appropriate to tip the server because you have taken up a table.

Should you go to the table to await your guest, don't order a drink or open your napkin. You want your guest to see a perfectly set table which implies that you just sat down. Stand as your guest approaches the table and remain standing until he or she is seated.

When you walk in together, let the guest precede you and be sure your guest is seated first in the best seat—the first one pulled out from the table by the captain, facing the room. If there is more than one guest, indicate their places and wait until they are seated before you sit. Whether the host is a woman or a man, the ranking guest gets the prime seat, the seat on the host's right.

When someone leaves the table briefly, it is not necessary for the host to stand. A man always has the option to stand when a woman leaves or joins the table, but today's businesswomen do not expect this at a business meal.

The Little Book of Etiquette

ORDERING DRINKS

Offer your guest a drink, even if you don't want one. Let the guest decide whether or not to drink alcohol. Order a drink if your guest does, although it does not have to be an alcoholic beverage. Explanations are not necessary.

ORDERING THE MEAL

Spend about five to ten minutes talking to allow you and your guest a chance to relax and establish a rapport with one another, and then request a menu. Don't just read the menu—talk through it with the server and ask about house specialties. Avoid putting your guest in the awkward position of not knowing the limits of your hospitality. Lightly suggest an appetizer you know is good and one of the more expensive items on the menu. Two suggestions are sufficient: "Ann, the food is delicious here, and I am partial to the grilled salmon and filet mignon." Your guest should not feel compelled to follow your suggestions, but she will get the message that such items are acceptable.

If your guest does order an appetizer or an expensive dish, you should too. Should the server forget and attempt to take your order first, simply indicate that your guest will order first.

*W*hen the meal is served, pay attention to the needs of your guest. You are the one responsible for signaling the server and requesting extra bread and butter, water, or whatever is wanted. Ask your guest if anything else is needed. Make all requests to servers in a businesslike manner and a normal tone of voice, prefaced with "please." Never express anger if the food or the service is unsatisfactory, but speak directly to the maître d' after you have said goodbye to your guest.

DISCUSSING BUSINESS

The primary focus of conversation at a business lunch should be business. After pleasantries (a good rule of thumb is to wait until the orders have been placed) you should say something that comfortably moves the conversation toward business. Your goal is to establish a relationship that ultimately leads to business. There should be only one or two items on your agenda, not a laundry list of topics. Focus on these items only, listening attentively, asking questions when necessary, reinforcing your areas of agreement, and determining the necessary follow-up steps.

CLOSING THE MEAL

At a business lunch it is important to respect your own time as well as that of your guest. There is simply no need to linger over your meal and allow the conversation to drift from your agenda. Use this time to review your discussion and decide on the appropriate action each of you will take.

Encourage your guest to have dessert when the server or captain returns with the dessert menu. If your guest orders dessert, you should too. If your guest only wants coffee, you should decline dessert and settle for the same.

PAYING THE BILL

When the coffee is served, request your check if prior arrangements were not made. Settle the bill quietly with your credit card. Check the bill for accuracy, but don't scrutinize it. Discrepancies should be handled after your guest leaves.

TIPPING

Tips are supposed to be a reward for services performed, as well as a supplement to an employee's income. According to legend, the word "tip" is derived from an innkeeper's sign "To Insure Promptness." If patrons deposited a few coins, they received their drinks faster.

Today the tip is given after a service is performed. It is the duty of the host to figure out the appropriate amount and never involve others at the table. Tipping in America is voluntary, and the amount is left up to the individual. Customs vary from one city to the next, depending on the area and elegance of the establishment. In other parts of the world, a preset percentage is added as a service charge.

The average gratuity is fifteen or twenty percent of the total bill (before taxes). A larger gratuity should be left for extraordinary food or service.

Should you be informed by management that you are the guest of the restaurant, it is still proper to leave a tip. You should leave at least 20 percent, with an additional ten to twenty dollars for the captain or server and twenty dollars for the maître d'.

The following rules generally apply at an upscale restaurant:

MAÎTRE D'/HOST—When you are a regular patron of a restaurant, tip ten to twenty dollars in cash depending on the size of your party and the level of service provided you.

CAPTAIN/HEADWAITER OR -WAITRESS—The person who takes your order receives 5 percent of the check.

SERVER—The person who serves your meal. The server receives 15 percent of the check, which is divided among all those involved in serving you. The bussers will share the tip and so will the bartender unless the bar bill is separate from your meal check.

SOMMELIER—The wine steward receives 10 percent of your wine bill. Tip 15 percent when the sommelier has helped you choose the best wine for the foods you have ordered.

COATROOM ATTENDANT—Leave one dollar for the first coat and fifty cents for each additional coat.

LEAVING

Escort your guest to the door and take care of the coats and other items you may have checked with the attendant. Shake hands and thank your guest for taking the time to join you for the meeting. Remind your guest of your next meeting, or if a date has not been set, promise to call within a few days.

GUEST DUTIES

It is the duty of the guest to thank the host, praise the choice of restaurant and food, and write a thank-you note. The best idea is to write the note as soon as you return to your office, so you will not have to worry about finding the time to perform this simple task. A short hand-written note on a correspondence card is all that is required: "Dorothea, I enjoyed the delicious lunch with you at Kincaid's and look forward to seeing your proposal on the International Protocol project we discussed. Considering our future expansion into the European market, this appears right on target. Many thanks,

Mark." Your host will admire your prompt and thoughtful reply.

A guest whose scrawl is illegible may, of course, send a typewritten note. Never fax or e-mail your thanks.

chapter seven

Forms

of Service

$\mathcal{S}$ervice describes the manner of presenting various dishes. Table service also takes into account the ensemble of objects used at the table: linens, plates, glasses, and silverware. The utensils required to serve a special function during the meal are called "services"—coffee service, tea service, dessert service, fruit service, etc.

The French also refer to the personnel of the restaurant who are responsible for serving meals as the "service."

Described herein are three classical forms of service common worldwide. The fourth form of service is used primarily in the United States of America.

SERVICE À LA FRANÇAISE—In the original French Service, all the dishes were set out in symmetrical patterns on the dining table and guests were expected to help themselves to dishes within their reach. This continued until the nineteenth century and is what we now call a buffet table.

SERVICE À LA RUSSE—In Russian Service, which replaced the original French Service, food is arranged on platters and passed by servers in a predetermined order to the guests, who may either help themselves or have food served to them.

*U*rban Dubois, a French food expert, originally popularized this service in the 1860s after visiting Russia and observing their style of dining. Originally, the chef decorated each dish, brought it to the dining salon, paraded it around the table, and then returned it to the kitchen for carving and service.

Today, service à la russe is simply referred to as French Service. In restaurants, this service employs a small serving table (guéridon) which is usually equipped with a side burner (réchaud). The captain or headwaiter presents the decorated meat, fish, poultry, game, or other dish in one piece on the platter, and then takes the dish to the serving table, where it is carved and served. This form of service is common in upscale restaurants worldwide.

SERVICE À L'ANGLAISE—In the English Service, a server presents the arranged platter from the left and serves the guest. This service is considered more economical and appropriate for banquets because a server can limit the portions served.

RESTAURANT OR AMERICAN STYLE—This form of service is used primarily in America. The food is placed on the plate in the kitchen and served directly to the diner. This service has the advantage of being fast, uncomplicated, and it does not require professional service.

In 1994, President and Mrs. Clinton replaced French Service (à la russe) at the White House with the Restaurant or American Style of service.

chapter eight

A FINAL WORD ON DINING ETIQUETTE

Dining can be a pleasurable experience when you are not frazzled by forks, nervous about napkins, or frightened by formalities. Polishing your dining skills need not be intimidating as long as you remember that learning is not a passive activity. Responsibility for results rests solely with you. It is a matter of commitment, common sense, home-work, and, most important, practice. Knowledge must become habit before it is truly useful. Don't wait until your next meal in a restaurant. Practice at home, while eating in a delicatessen, or at a fast-food restaurant. Practice until the process is automatic. Then you will not become overwhelmed by numerous details when you need your skills the most. Should you forget what to do at some point dur-ing the meal, relax. Consider your next logical or practical move, as well as what seems the most refined—and then do it. As soon as you get home, you can check yourself against your *Little Book of Etiquette* and do the correct thing the next time. Fait accompli!

*S*hould you wish to study etiquette in more detail, you may also want to contact the Protocol School of Washington®.

The Protocol School of Washington®
International Headquarters
1401 Chain Bridge Road, Suite 202
McLean, Virginia 22101

A Final Word

As the nation's leading etiquette and protocol consulting firm, the Protocol School of Washington® offers seminars that show you how to handle all situations where business is promoted and discussed. Whatever your choice, you should feel confident that you now have the basic tools to handle yourself with class in any dining situation.

This book has been bound using
handcraft methods, and Smyth-sewn
to ensure durability.

The dust jacket was designed
by Diane Miljat.

The interior was designed
by Nancy Loggins Gonzalez.

The dust jacket and interior were
illustrated by Denise Hilton-Campbell.

The text was edited by Elaine M. Bucher.

The text was set in Granjon with
Shelley Volante Script.